The Essential Guide to ADHD

Maintaining Mental Well-Being

Table of Contents

Chapter 1. Introduction

Welcome to "The Essential Guide to ADHD: Maintaining Mental Well-Being" - your definitive compass to maneuvering the complexities of ADHD with positivity, resilience, and hope. This Special Report not only delves into the intricacies of ADHD but more importantly, it illuminates your path towards mental well-being. You'll gain access to practical, insightful strategies designed to empower you or your loved ones, with comprehensive coverage ranging from understanding the condition, debunking common misconceptions, treatment approaches to self-care techniques. By the end of this exciting guide, you'll be firmly in the driver's seat, ready to shape your mental well-being journey with newfound knowledge and confidence. So, why wait? This is your moment to take an invigorating leap towards a life that understands ADHD in its entirety and heralds mental well-being. Grab your copy of this special report today, and let's embark on this enlightening adventure together!

Chapter 2. Demystifying ADHD: An Essential Overview

Attention-Deficit/Hyperactivity Disorder (ADHD) is a common neurodevelopmental disorder, often diagnosed in childhood but can continue through adolescence towards adulthood. Despite its prevalence, it is often misunderstood - painted across a canvas of stereotypes and misconceptions. To truly understand ADHD, it is imperative to delve into the scientific underpinnings and dispel the myths that surround it.

2.1. Unraveling the Root: The Science Behind ADHD

ADHD is primarily associated with the brain's frontal lobes, which control executive functions such as attention, memory, emotional regulation, and decision-making. Neuroimaging studies suggest differences in the size and activity level of certain brain structures in individuals with ADHD, particularly the prefrontal cortex and basal ganglia.

Researchers have identified several neurotransmitters, specifically dopamine and norepinephrine, which play a vital role in executive functioning, as key to the manifestation of ADHD symptoms. Inadequate production or inefficient utilization of these chemicals can lead to complications in concentration, organization, and impulse control, elements that define ADHD.

In addition to this, genetics also weigh heavily on the ADHD causality scale. Findings suggest a significant hereditary link, with the likelihood of occurrence being higher in individuals who have a relative diagnosed with the condition.

2.2. Brushing Off the Myths

ADHD, despite its clinical and research-driven history, is often misinterpreted, leading to widespread myths that create barriers in understanding and managing the condition.

The first misconception is that ADHD is a hallmark of childhood and dissipates over time. While it does often commence in childhood, many continue to experience symptoms into adulthood. A shift in symptoms' nature may occur with age – hyperactivity may dampen, for instance, but issues with attention or impulsivity may persist.

Another common myth is that ADHD only affects males. Statistics show males being diagnosed more frequently; however, this disparity is attributed to differences in symptom manifestation. Girls often exhibit inattentive symptoms, which can be easily overlooked compared to hyperactive symptoms, more commonly seen in boys.

It is also falsely claimed that people with ADHD cannot succeed in academic or professional landscapes. Individuals with ADHD possess unique strengths like creativity, adaptability, and problem-solving, which, when combined with effective management strategies, contribute significantly to their success.

2.3. Understanding the Symptomatology

The American Psychiatric Association's Diagnostic and Statistical Manual (DSM-5) recognizes three types of ADHD: predominately inattentive presentation, predominately hyperactive-impulsive presentation, and combined presentation.

Inattention is characterized by difficulty sustaining focus, chronic disorganization, forgetfulness, and a propensity towards being easily distracted. Hyperactivity, on the other hand, is seen in behaviors such as excessive fidgeting, restlessness, and impulsivity associated with difficulty waiting turns or speaking out of turn.

It's important to remember that these symptoms can vary by an individual's age and surrounding environment. For example, an adult may exhibit less hyperactivity but struggle with attention and organization in their daily responsibilities.

2.4. Approaching Diagnosis

ADHD diagnosis is an intricate process that involves comprehensive evaluations to rule out other potential conditions, determining if symptoms are long-standing and disruptive to daily life, as well as if they stem from at least two different settings such as home and school.

For children, diagnostic standards require the manifestation of several symptoms before age 12. For adults, standards are less rigid, acknowledging that exact childhood symptoms may not be accurately recalled. In such cases, evidence of ongoing symptoms is critical.

2.5. Treating ADHD: Going Beyond Medication

Treatment for ADHD often involves a multifaceted approach. While medications, such as stimulants, do play a significant role in managing symptoms by regulating brain chemistry, they are not the solitary solution.

Behavioral therapy, for both children and adults with ADHD, can be instrumental in teaching and reinforcing desired behaviors while reducing problematic ones. Skills training can help manage challenging tasks and responsibilities, while parental training can provide tools necessary to guide a child with ADHD effectively.

For adults, cognitive-behavioral therapy (CBT) often proves beneficial, focusing on altering unhelpful thought patterns, developing coping mechanisms, and improving organizational skills.

To conclude, ADHD is a nuanced condition, characterized by diversity in its manifestation, pathway, and treatment response. But with awareness, a commitment to understanding, and a compassionate perspective, it is not a condition to fear. Rather, it is a part of the fabric of one's being, which can be worn proudly, with hope, resilience, and positivity.

Chapter 3. Deciphering the Symptoms: Recognizing ADHD

ADHD, or Attention Deficit Hyperactivity Disorder, is a complex neurodevelopmental disorder often diagnosed in childhood but that can persist into adulthood. Characterized by patterns of inattention, hyperactivity, and impulsive behavior that hinder daily functioning, ADHD can impact both academic and professional achievement and can affect personal relationships. Recognizing the symptoms is the first step towards understanding this condition and seeking help.

3.1. Understanding ADHD

ADHD is considered a neurodevelopmental disorder as, in most cases, it begins in early childhood and continues into adulthood. While the causes of ADHD are still the subject of scientific research, it is believed to result from a combination of genetic, environmental, and neurological factors.

Individuals with ADHD may exhibit different types of symptoms: primarily inattentive, primarily hyperactive/impulsive, or a combination of both. Inattention refers to difficulty maintaining focus, especially on tasks that require prolonged mental effort. Hyperactivity denotes excessive movement or activity, particularly in situations where such behavior is inappropriate. Impulsivity refers to making hasty, inconsiderate decisions without considering the potential consequences.

3.2. Inattention

Many people occasionally struggle with inattention in specific settings. Yet, for individuals with ADHD, these symptoms can be chronic and pervasive, affecting various aspects of their lives. Symptoms included under inattention are:

1. Difficulty maintaining focus on tasks or play activities

2. Easily sidetracked, and failure to finish schoolwork, chores, or workplace duties

3. Overlooking details and making careless mistakes when at school or work

4. Appearing not to listen when spoken to directly

5. Failing to follow instructions, and difficulty organizing tasks and activities

6. Lacking persistence, quickly being frustrated by tasks that require continuous mental effort

7. Often losing things required for tasks, like pencils, books, or tools

8. Being easily distracted by unrelated thoughts or stimuli

9. Frequently forgetting to do everyday activities such as chores or assignments

3.3. Hyperactivity and Impulsivity

Hyperactivity and impulsivity are two tightly intertwined facets of ADHD and often manifest together. These behaviors generally appear before the age of seven, although they may go unnoticed in early childhood because they can be misinterpreted as typical child behavior. Below are the common signs of hyperactivity and impulsivity:

1. Frequently fidgeting or squirming

2. Leaving their seats in situations where staying seated is expected (e.g., in school)

3. Running around and climbing in inappropriate situations, in the case of young children

4. Having difficulty playing or partaking in leisure activities quietly

5. Often appearing "on the go" or acting as though "driven by a motor"

6. Talking excessively

7. Interrupting or intruding on others (for example, butting into conversations, games, or activities)

8. Having difficulty waiting in a queue or taking turns

3.4. ADHD in Adults

While the symptoms of ADHD often start in childhood, they may continue for many adolescents and adults. For some adults, ADHD may not have been diagnosed during childhood, leaving them unaware of why they face certain struggles. Symptoms of ADHD in adults can include the following problems:

1. Chronic lateness and forgetfulness

2. Anxiety

3. Low self-esteem

4. Problems at work

5. Trouble controlling anger

6. Impulsiveness

7. Substance abuse or addiction

8. Unorganized

9. Procrastination

10. Easily frustrated

11. Chronic boredom

12. Trouble concentrating when reading

13. Mood swings

14. Depression

15. Relationship problems

These symptoms may vary widely among adults and can contribute to a number of related problems, like inconsistent performance at work or frequent job changes, substance abuse, vehicular accidents, and other risky behaviors.

3.5. Getting a Diagnosis

It's important to note that only trained healthcare providers, such as pediatricians, psychologists, or psychiatrists, can provide ADHD diagnoses. Their evaluation will include a comprehensive investigation that takes into account symptom history, observed behavior, and mental status examinations. ADHD cannot be diagnosed through a single test. Instead, the healthcare provider uses several different types of assessments and observations to make an accurate diagnosis. These may include questionnaires, behavior observation, interview, and clinical history.

If you or a loved one are experiencing symptoms of ADHD, it is crucial to seek help from a mental health professional. A diagnosis can be a critical step towards obtaining appropriate treatment and support, leading to improvements in qualities of life and a better understanding of this complex condition.

In the journey to managing ADHD, knowledge is indeed power. Being aware of and recognizing the symptoms paves the way for assistance, coping mechanisms, and a fruitful life—a life that navigates ADHD with resilience, positivity, and hope.

Remember that every journey begins with the first step, and understanding ADHD is an essential start. Acknowledging symptoms not only demystifies ADHD but also helps set the stage for treatment options and fostering positive mental well-being. As we journey through this guide, you will find yourself gaining more knowledge and understanding, aiding your efforts to bridge the knowledge gap of ADHD and to embrace mental well-being fully.

Chapter 4. Realizing Impacts: ADHD in Daily Life

At the heart of our understanding of ADHD is the tangible impacts it has on our daily lives. Whether you are living with ADHD, or care for someone who is, clear awareness of these impacts is the first critical step towards managing them.

4.1. Recognizing ADHD: Different Manifestations

ADHD can manifest in a variety of ways. Impulsivity, hyperactivity, and inattentiveness are the three key characteristics commonly associated with the condition. However, these can present differently among those affected. For example, while some may predominantly exhibit hyperactivity, others might show primarily inattentive symptoms. Recognizing these distinctive features can aid in the construction of a management plan suited to your unique needs.

Understanding how these traits intertwine with your routine holds immense significance. You could find yourself struggling with maintaining focus throughout a project, often missing the minutiae. Perhaps you notice an uncontrolled urge to move, to the point where it distracts from your task at hand. For those leaning more towards impulsivity, making hasty decisions without the typical deliberation might be a frequent occurrence.

4.2. Significance of Early Detection

Early detection of these traits can be a game-changer in how you navigate life with ADHD. Acknowledging the symptom, particularly while they're in their initial stages, brings you one step closer to forming a proactive approach that minimizes its disruptive influence on your daily endeavors.

Four key areas are often affected by ADHD, which if preemptively addressed, can significantly improve the quality of life.

1. School/work performance: This is arguably the most noticeable field of impact. Struggling with focus and attention often interferes with the completion of tasks, leading to disappointing grades or performance reviews.

2. Social interactions: Impulsivity and hyperactivity may make it challenging to socialize. Engaging in conversations might feel difficult; interrupting others, expressing thoughts rapidly or restlessly jumping between topics is common.

3. Self-esteem: Regular confrontations with these challenges often lead to feelings of inadequacy and a lower sense of self-worth.

4. Mental health: Over time, these experiences can translate into stress, anxiety, and even depression.

4.3. Living with ADHD: From Chaos to Control

Transitioning from recognizing ADHD's impact on daily life to navigating these challenges can seem daunting. However, employing certain techniques and strategies can ease this process significantly.

Time management is a powerful tool when wielded correctly. Structuring your day with set routines brings order to the otherwise perceived chaos. Simple habits such as using planners, setting up reminders, or blocking your day into concrete tasks can alleviate the stress of feeling unorganized.

Ensuring a well-balanced diet and regular exercise has shown to bear positive results. Physical activity contributes towards boosting focus and stabilizing mood swings, while a nutritious diet can assist in maintaining overall brain function.

Finally, setting achievable goals and celebrating the minor victories can uplift your mood and motivate you to continue progressing.

4.4. The Unseen Struggle: It's More than "Just Difficulty Focusing"

ADHD isn't just about having trouble paying attention or being 'too active'. It is a condition that weaves itself into the fabric of your daily life, affecting various aspects that outsiders may not see or understand. Feelings of being misunderstood or dismissed can lead to a sense of isolation. Remember, it's not about fitting into the world without ADHD; it's about creating a world that understands and adapts to ADHD.

4.5. Conclusion: Recognizing, Understanding, and Adapting

The profound daily impacts of ADHD are undeniable. They permeate every facet of life, varying in appearance and intensity. Yet, it's vital to remember that acknowledgment is the first step towards transformation. With understanding comes the power to adapt, enabling you to navigate through the maze of challenges with resilience and hope.

Endeavor to accept yourself unconditionally. Everyone has unique struggles, and it's okay to fumble and learn. Being patient and practicing self-care, coupled with the knowledge you've gathered about ADHD's impacts, can ultimately lead you to a fulfilling life. Remember, you are not alone. Together, we can illuminate the path towards understanding this fascinating condition and promoting mental wellbeing. Your journey might feel winding and infinite, but with tailored strategies, abundant resources, and a supportive community, nothing is out of reach.

Chapter 5. The Science Behind ADHD: Understanding the Neuroscience

Attention-Deficit/Hyperactivity Disorder (ADHD) is one of the most commonly diagnosed neurological disorders in children, often persisting in the individual's adulthood. It's characterized by persistent patterns of inattention, hyperactivity, and impulsivity. The examination of the science behind ADHD is a relatively new field of study, but various researches in neuroscience have provided strides in our understanding of this disorder.

5.1. The Brain and ADHD

The human brain is an incredibly complex organ, made up of billions of neurons that create and decode an unparalleled number of connections. To understand ADHD, one must comprehend the relevance of these connections. Neurotransmitters, chemical substances responsible for transmitting signals across a neural gap called a synapse, play an integral role in modulating human thoughts, emotions, and behavior.

For a person with ADHD, the production, delivery, and standardized function of these neurotransmitters are disrupted, particularly those of dopamine and norepinephrine. These neurotransmitters are crucial for attention and impulse control, cognitive functions. These disparities in biochemical mechanisms result in the distinctive behavioral traits observed in ADHD.

5.2. Variations in ADHD Brains

Neuroimaging technologies, such as MRI and PET scans, have

revealed significant differences between the brains of individuals with ADHD and those without. A meta-analysis of MRI studies have concluded that those with ADHD tend to have slightly smaller total brain volumes with most consistent reductions found within the frontal lobes, basal ganglia, and cerebellum. Especially, the prefrontal cortex, involved in attention regulation and impulse control, shows significant underactivity. The basal ganglia, a group of nuclei linked through neurons responsible for reward functioning, is also lesser in volume.

5.3. Genetic Factors of ADHD

Just as the answer to most biological mysteries, the factor underlying these neuronal and structural variations is genetic. Twin studies and recent advances in DNA technology have given compelling evidence that ADHD is highly heritable. Certain genes, such as DRD4 and DAT1, implicated in the dopamine pathway, have been highlighted. Though no single "ADHD gene" has been discovered, research continues to affirm the complex genetic underpinnings, and possibly the interplay of multiple genes, the environment, and their interactions contributing to the disorder's development.

5.4. ADHD and Comorbidity: A Neuroscience Perspective

Data suggests that ADHD seldomly occurs in isolation, frequently accompanied by one or more comorbid disorders, including anxiety, depressive disorders, or learning disabilities, making ADHD's etiology more complex. These comorbidities further complicate the brain's neural architecture and reflect in overlapping, confusing symptoms. Understanding this shared neurobiology can fashion more holistic diagnostic procedures and treatment techniques.

5.5. Evolving Understanding of ADHD

The exploration into ADHD does not end here. Though we have come a long way in integrating our understanding of ADHD from a neurological and genetic perspective, it's also crucial to remember that our knowledge remains in its nascent stages. The interplay of genes and environment, the role of epigenetics, detailing of neurotransmitter activity, and its relationship to behavioral symptoms are still wider areas that demand exploration.

In conclusion, ADHD is a genetic, neurobiological disorder, linked to structural changes within the brain, disturbances in neurotransmitter activities, and at the same time influenced by combined genetic and environmental influences. This broad understanding, however, only skims the surface of the intricacies of ADHD, and the quest to fully comprehend this complex disorder is ever-continuing.

Our understanding, powered by relentless research, has already resulted in better diagnostic techniques and more targeted interventions, facilitating those struggling with ADHD to manage their symptoms and live fulfilling lives. The hope is that, as scientific understanding continues to evolve, we will uncover more effective approaches to foster well-being among those with ADHD. Despite the complexities, the progress made to date confirms that an enlightened pathway to mental health is possible.

Chapter 6. Mental Health & ADHD: The Significant Interplay

When we first consider any discussion around Attention-Deficit/Hyperactivity Disorder (ADHD), it's essential to recognize its significant connection to our mental health. ADHD isn't merely about an inability to focus or hyperactivity. It's a neurodevelopmental disorder intricately interwoven with our mental and emotional reservoir.

6.1. The Layered Connection

The ADHD experience isn't a monolith. It manifests differently in every individual, making the interplay with mental health extremely multifaceted. Mental health disorders, like anxiety or depression, can come off as a sidecar to ADHD. It might emerge as a direct result of the challenges in handling ADHD, or it might exist independently, creating a complex maze that needs careful attention.

ADHD can throw everyday tasks into chaos. Difficulty in maintaining schedules, remembering details, completing tasks, or impulsivity can create a domino effect disrupting personal and professional relationships. This can plunge individuals into an abyss of self-doubt and discontent, fueling mental disorders like chronic anxiety, depression, or even bipolar disorder.

ADHD symptoms can often become amplified by external environments. A schoolkid might struggle to keep pace in a rigid, structured educational setting, affecting grades and self-esteem. Adults might find it challenging to meet expectations at work or indulge in impulsive decisions leading to financial instability. Such cumulative stress can create a breeding ground for mental health disorders.

6.2. The Coinciding Disorders

According to multiple studies, nearly 50% of adults with ADHD also have an anxiety disorder. Other frequent travelers include depression, bipolar disorder, and obsessive-compulsive disorder. People battling ADHD and such conditions often feel they are locked in a continuous struggle, where one seems to perpetually feed the other.

For instance, the persistent worry associated with an anxiety disorder can exacerbate the difficulty with concentration in ADHD. On the other hand, the inability to focus might lead to added stress and fuel anxiety. That's why these conditions need to be treated as intertwined rather than isolated disorders.

6.3. Understanding Comorbidity

Comorbidity - the simultaneous presence of two or more chronic illnesses or conditions in a person- is a common feature with ADHD. It is estimated that 60% to 80% of children and adults with ADHD have at least one other psychiatric disorder.

Why such high rates of comorbidity? Certain brain structures and processes involved in ADHD also play a role in these other psychiatric conditions. It's like being vulnerable to a group of disorders, and depending on other factors like genetics or life events, you might develop one or more of these conditions. Comorbidity is a critical part of understanding ADHD and shouldn't be overlooked during diagnosis and treatment.

6.4. The Importance of Accurate Diagnosis

Accurate diagnosis gears treatment in the right direction. One of the main challenges in diagnosing ADHD with co-existing mental health disorders is their overlapping symptoms. For instance, restlessness and difficulty in focusing are common between ADHD and anxiety. Depression and ADHD can share symptoms like disorganized thought process or forgetfulness. So, it's no surprise that ADHD often gets misdiagnosed as other conditions and vice versa.

A comprehensive diagnostic assessment includes a detailed review of the symptoms, their duration, when they first appeared, and in which settings they occur. It's also useful to gather information from various sources, like the individual, family members, teachers (in case of children), or coworkers. A thorough diagnostic assessment eases the way for effective treatment strategies.

6.5. Tailoring Suitable Treatment Plans

Treatment for comorbid ADHD and mental health disorders often involves a mix of medication, psychotherapy, behavior interventions, and self-care measures. Pharmacological treatments may include stimulants, non-stimulants, antidepressants, or a combination depending on the nature and intensity of the symptoms.

Cognitive-behavioral therapy (CBT) encourages skills to manage symptoms or modify behavior patterns that cause problems. For instance, CBT could help mitigate feelings of worthlessness common in depression or develop strategies to reign in impulsivity associated with ADHD.

Behavioral interventions like creating organized, predictable environments or breaking tasks into simpler, manageable chunks can be beneficial.

And lastly, self-care measures, like a balanced diet, regular physical activity, adequate sleep, and mindfulness, can go a long way in managing ADHD and mental health disorders.

6.6. Building Resilience: The Ultimate Armor

Living with ADHD and mental health disorders can feel like an uphill battle. Yet, many individuals learn to thrive despite these challenges. The key lies in resilience - the ability to cope with adversity and bounce back.

Building resilience starts with accepting your unique brain wiring rather than fighting it. It involves focusing on strengths and utilizing them better. Harnessing a growth mindset can transform challenges into opportunities for learning. Cultivating a positive self-image, practicing self-compassion, developing coping skills, and fostering supportive relationships are indispensable elements in the resilience armory.

Remember, ADHD isn't an insurmountable barrier; it's merely a different perspective. With the right strategies and supports, you can navigate the mental health-ADHD interplay, transforming your challenges into unique strengths and leading a fulfilling, prosperous life.

Chapter 7. ADHD Treatments: Medical and Therapeutic Approaches

ADHD, also known as Attention-Deficit Hyperactivity Disorder, is a neurological condition that significantly affects an individual's ability to control their behavior, focus and maintain attention, or a combination of these symptoms.

Understanding that each person with ADHD is unique and requires personalized treatment plans is crucial. There is a wide range of treatments available, from medication management to therapeutic approaches aimed at improving symptoms and quality of life. We will decipher these various options in detail, offering you an insightful understanding of ADHD treatment.

7.1. Medication

Medication is often a key part of treatment for ADHD. There are primarily two types of medications used: stimulants and non-stimulants.

Stimulant medications are generally the first line of treatment for ADHD. They include drugs like methylphenidate (Ritalin, Concerta) and amphetamines (Adderall). These medications work by increasing the availability of certain chemicals in the brain, thereby helping to enhance focus and attention, and reduce impulsivity and hyperactivity.

Non-stimulant medications, like atomoxetine (Strattera), clonidine (Kapvay), and guanfacine (Intuniv), can be beneficial when stimulant medications are ineffective or cause significant side effects. Unlike stimulant medication, non-stimulants work by regulating neurotransmitters, leading to a decrease in ADHD symptoms.

When considering medication, it's crucial to have an open conversation with your healthcare provider about the potential benefits, side effects, and the appropriate dosage. Regular check-ups are critical to monitor progress and make necessary adjustments to the treatment plan.

7.2. Psychotherapy

Beyond medication, psychotherapy plays a crucial role in treating ADHD. Therapy options may include Cognitive Behavioral Therapy (CBT), family therapy, or social skills training.

Cognitive Behavioral Therapy (CBT) involves working with a mental health professional to develop strategies for managing behaviors associated with ADHD. It aims to help individuals overcome difficulties by changing negative thought patterns and enhancing problem-solving skills.

Family therapy may be beneficial for improving the family environment and interactions, particularly in cases where ADHD has influenced family dynamics.

Social skills training focuses on teaching individuals with ADHD how to interact more effectively and comfortably with peers and adults. It can also help improve their ability to understand social cues, manage frustration, and deal with criticism.

7.3. Behavioral Interventions

Behavioral interventions are practical approaches focused on modifying behavior through systematic methods. Some of these interventions include behavioral therapy, classroom interventions, and parent management training.

Behavioral therapy involves learning new behaviors to replace behaviors that are causing problems. It is often used in combination with medication, especially for managing symptoms in school settings.

Classroom interventions involve making changes to a child's school environment to help them maintain focus and achieve academic success. This might include seating arrangements, additional breaks, or an adjusted workload.

Parent management training equips parents with techniques to help their children manage symptoms and behaviors. Strategies might include using rewards or penalties, establishing routines, or applying consistent discipline practices.

7.4. Lifestyle and Home Remedies

ADHD can also be managed with certain lifestyle changes and home remedies. Regular exercise, an organized living environment, and a balanced diet can make a significant difference.

Regular physical activity can help improve symptoms of ADHD by increasing the brain's dopamine, norepinephrine, and serotonin levels – which affect focus and attention.

An organized living environment, with clear rules and routines, can help individuals with ADHD function better and decrease feelings of chaos and disorder.

Finally, a balanced diet can contribute positively to brain function and behavior. While no specific food has been shown to improve ADHD symptoms, a nutritious diet—one rich in proteins, fruits, vegetables, and whole grains with limited sugar and junk food—can aid overall mental and physical well-being.

Understanding the various aspects of ADHD treatment can empower you to make an informed decision about what route to take. Remember, there's no one-size-fits-all treatment for ADHD, and what works best will depend on the individual. Through careful observation, patient trial and error, and open conversations with healthcare providers, you can find the right combination of treatments that best supports you or your loved ones. Remember, understanding ADHD and maintaining mental well-being is a journey, and each step forward, no matter how small, is progress.

Chapter 8. Positive Parenting Strategies for Children with ADHD

Navigating the tumultuous journey of parenting can be doubly challenging when your child has ADHD (Attention Deficit Hyperactivity Disorder). The unique dynamics that ADHD brings can sometimes leave parents feeling overwhelmed and under-equipped, but with the right approach and strategies, it is possible to overcome these hurdles and foster a positive environment for your child.

8.1. Understanding Your Child's ADHD

Before diving right into the parenting strategies, it's essential to have a comprehensive understanding of your child's ADHD. Essentially, kids with ADHD may have trouble paying attention, controlling impulsive behaviors, or being overly active. However, like any other condition, ADHD varies extensively from one child to another, reflecting a broad spectrum of symptoms, strengths, and experiences.

The areas frequently impacted by ADHD include attention, impulsivity, hyperactivity, executive function, and emotional regulation. By understanding each facet, we can tailor the best strategies to encourage positive practices in our children.

8.2. Tailoring Communication

Effective communication makes up the cornerstone of any parenting strategy for kids with ADHD. It involves speaking clearly, listening keenly, and responding aptly to your child's needs.

Use short, simple, and direct sentences when communicating with your child. Provide instructions one at a time and be consistent with your language. Avoiding complex language limits the chances of misunderstanding, ensuring your message is effectively passed.

Consider low-tech communication solutions such as visual aids. These can often serve as a powerful tool for children with ADHD as it helps outline tasks, provides a tangible reminder, and fosters independence.

Active listening is just as crucial. Ensure your child feels heard and validated. This can significantly improve their self-esteem and cultivate a positive child-parent relationship.

8.3. Creating Structure and Routine

Children with ADHD often thrive in a structured, efficient environment where their day is mapped out for them. This predictability offers them a sense of security and comfort and helps them to better manage their behavior and time.

Make sure to establish set times for meals, homework, play, and bedtime. Use visual schedules and charts to help your child understand what to expect each day.

8.4. Using Positive Reinforcement

Positive reinforcement is a potent tool in guiding your child's behavior. Reward and acknowledge good behavior when you see it. This can be in the form of praise, hugs, or tangible rewards.

Build a system where your child can earn privileges or rewards for good behavior. This enhances their motivation and encourages them to repeat these behaviors.

8.5. Encouraging Physical Activity

Physical activity has been shown to reduce symptoms of ADHD. Encourage your child to take part in active play daily, and consider enrolling them in organized sports or activities that they are interested in.

8.6. Assisting with Sleep Issues

Sleep disturbances are common among children with ADHD. This can exacerbate their symptoms and make them more challenging to manage. Establishing a consistent, relaxing bedtime routine can greatly aid in improving sleep quality.

Avoid screens for at least an hour before bed, ensure their sleep environment is comforting, and use white noise machines or weighted blankets if you think your child may benefit from them.

8.7. Balancing Diet and Nutrition

While there isn't a specific food that can neatly 'cure' ADHD, certain dietary changes can help manage the symptoms. Be sure to provide a varied, nutritious diet rich in fruits, vegetables, lean proteins, and whole grains. Limit food and drinks with high amounts of added sugars.

8.8. Teaching Social Skills

Children with ADHD sometimes struggle with social situations. Role-playing different scenarios at home can be a tremendous help. Provide them with tools and strategies for interacting in various settings, and openly discuss their strengths and areas for improvement.

8.9. Working Collaboratively with Teachers

School plays a big part in your child's life, making it crucial to maintain an open line of communication with their teachers. Share helpful strategies, discuss recurring problems, and collaborate on a consistent approach to behavioral management.

8.10. Practicing Self-Care

Parenting a child with ADHD can indeed be stressful. Be sure to take time for self-care to recharge and unwind. Pursue hobbies, get together with friends or simply take a quiet moment for yourself. Remember, the most effective parenting comes from a place of emotional well-being.

8.11. Seeking Professional Help

If your child's symptoms persist or worsen despite your efforts, it may be time to seek professional help. This could involve working with a child psychologist or psychiatrist, occupational therapist, or ADHD coach.

In conclusion, while parenting a child with ADHD presents its own set of challenges, deploying effective strategies can lead to positive outcomes. The key lies in understanding your child's unique needs, being patient, consistent, and being responsive to changing dynamics. There is no one-size-fits-all solution, only a journey of discovery to find what works best for your child.

Chapter 9. Life Hacks: Managing Adult ADHD at Work and Home

ADHD, attention-deficit/hyperactivity disorder, influences every facet of your life. From personal relationships to professional duties, managing this condition can be a daunting task. However, understanding how ADHD affects adults can provide the stepping stones to lead a healthier, more organized and balanced life. Let's dive into various strategies and techniques that can essentially aid you in managing ADHD at work and home, ensuring smooth sails ahead.

9.1. Understanding ADHD

Noticeable in early childhood, ADHD symptoms often extend to adulthood. Symptoms may vary from person to person, but common ones include impulsivity, difficulty maintaining attention, and hyperactivity. However, these behaviors are often less overt in adults than in children.

ADHD is not simply a label but rather a detailed explanation towards certain patterns of behavior. Research has shown that ADHD is largely hereditary. Missed or misdiagnosed during childhood, you might carry the condition into adulthood, not knowing the root cause of your struggles with organization, consistency, and focus.

9.2. Building Structure and Routine

Anxiety and stress often stem from unpredictable situations. Incorporating a structured routine in your day-to-day life can offer predictability and help alleviate ADHD symptoms. Create a detailed schedule and follow it diligently. This process manifests a sense of accomplishment that plays a crucial role in boosting and maintaining your motivation.

Example: Establish wakeup and bedtimes, include time slots for meals, breaks, leisure activities, and exercise.

9.3. Effective Time Management Skills

Utilize visual cues to manage your time more effectively. Wall clocks, timers, and alarms are all beneficial in keeping track of time. You can also set alarms to notify you of the start and finish of tasks.

Technology can be your ally too! Apps for reminders, time management, and list-making can help create a seamless work routine. Remember, the goal is to simplify your life, not to complicate it, so employ tools that make sense for you and are easily manageable.

9.4. Organizing Task Management

Break down projects into smaller, achievable tasks. "Chunk" your work to make it less overwhelming and more manageable. This approach avoids confusion and leads to more productive outcomes.

Remember to prioritize your tasks. Tackling high-priority tasks when you are highly energetic can lead to increased productivity and efficiency.

9.5. Creating a Distraction-Free Work Environment

An organized, clutter-free workspace contributes to increased attention and productivity. Create an environment that minimally distracts you. This might involve having tidy workspaces both at home and in the office.

Implement tools such as white-noise machines or noise-canceling headphones. If possible, have a dedicated quiet area to work from to promote concentration.

9.6. Acquiring Coping Strategies

Various coping strategies can be helpful in workplace environments, such as:

1. Seeking out appropriate coaching or mentoring.

2. Requesting written instructions whenever possible.

3. Using techniques for managing stress, such as mindfulness, relaxation, and regular exercises.

4. Keeping a notebook or digital note-taking app to jot down essential points and tasks to avoid forgetting.

5. Sharing your condition with trusted colleagues for support – not all workplaces are understanding, so careful consideration is required before sharing.

9.7. Managing Family and Relationships

ADHD can also impact personal relationships. Active communication plays a vital role here. Be open about your condition, allowing your family and friends to better understand you and provide supportive environments.

Develop a habit of writing down important events, birthdays, and anniversaries. Use in-daily planners or smartphone apps to alert you. These strides help in avoiding misunderstandings and keeping healthy relationships.

9.8. Self-Care: Mental and Physical Wellness

A nutrient-rich diet, physical activities, and sufficient rest are crucial for managing ADHD. Regular exercises boost your mood, improve sleep, decrease anxiety, and promote a sense of wellbeing.

Maintaining a consistent bedtime routine is also essential. Set a winding-down routine to signal your body for relaxation and rest. This could be calming activities like reading or listening to soft music.

9.9. Seeking Professional Help

Consult a mental health professional if you find your symptoms interfering with your quality of life. Therapies such as Cognitive Behavioral Therapy (CBT) have proven effective for adults with ADHD. CBT helps in identifying harmful patterns of thought and teaches how to replace them with healthier ones.

Remember, you're not alone on your journey with ADHD. By leveraging the right tactics, tools, and treatments, you can navigate the complexities of ADHD, both at work and at home. With these life hacks in your arsenal, you have a clear pathway to enhancing productivity, fostering healthy relationships, and championing mental well-being. Your ADHD doesn't define you - you hold the power to redefine how it influences your life. Choose empowerment. Choose resilience. Choose living well.

Chapter 10. Nourishing Resilience: Self-Care Tips for People with ADHD

Taking care of oneself is important for everyone but when you have ADHD, it becomes even more significant. Self-care is not just about physical well-being; it's about nurturing your mental, emotional, and spiritual well-being too. It's about recognizing your needs and taking the necessary steps to meet them. Here are some self-care tips specially designed for individuals with ADHD to foster resilience and promote well-being.

10.1. Understand the Impact of Diet

"A healthy diet is a solution to many of our health-care problems. It's the most important solution." – John Mackey, Co-founder and CEO of Whole Foods Market

Your brain needs a mix of nutrients to function optimally and this becomes extremely crucial when dealing with ADHD. Both adequate nutrition and debarring certain food items play a central role in managing ADHD symptoms.

Complex carbohydrates like whole grains, fruits, vegetables, and legumes digest slowly, providing you with stable energy levels. Protein-rich foods such as lean meat, legumes, and dairy products increase the production of neurotransmitters, which are essential for attention and focus. Omega-3 fatty acids like those found in fatty fish, flax seeds, and walnuts, have been shown to reduce ADHD symptoms as they play a key role in brain function.

Observing your diet and identifying any food items that tend to aggravate your symptoms can be beneficial. Some individuals with

ADHD are sensitive to food additives, caffeine, or sugar causing an escalation in symptoms. An elimination trial, supervised by a dietician or a healthcare provider, can help determine any potential adverse food reactions.

10.2. Invest in Physical Activity

Physical activity is stimulating for the brain. Regular exercise can increase the level of brain chemicals like dopamine, serotonin, and norepinephrine, which are critical in regulating mood and behavior.

For individuals with ADHD, adopting a regular exercise routine can help reduce impulsivity, improve concentration, enhance memory, and alleviate depressive symptoms. Whether it's brisk walking, dancing, yoga, or team sports, find a physical activity that you enjoy and make it part of your daily routine. When exercise becomes a pleasure rather than a chore, you're more likely to stick with it.

10.3. Prioritize Restful Sleep

Sleep is restorative to the brain. However, ADHD sometimes makes it challenging to establish a healthy sleep pattern. Insufficient sleep tends to exacerbate ADHD symptoms like inattentiveness, impulsivity, and mood swings.

Try adhering to the following practices to improve your sleep. Establish a consistent sleep schedule by waking up and retiring to bed at the same time every day–even on weekends. Make sure your bedroom is dark, quiet, and cool. Limit screen time at least an hour before bed to reduce exposure to blue light that can disrupt your sleep cycle. Practice mindful relaxation techniques like deep breathing, progressive muscle relaxation, or listen to calming music.

10.4. Discover Mindfulness

Mindfulness is the practice of focusing one's conscious awareness on the present moment, while calmly acknowledging and accepting one's feelings, thoughts, and bodily sensations.

Incorporating mindfulness in your daily routine can be particularly beneficial for people with ADHD. It aids to slow the mind, improve focus, reduce impulsivity, and foster emotional balance. Practice mindfulness through meditation, yoga, or simply taking a few minutes every day to sit in silence, focusing on your breath or the sounds around you.

10.5. Establish Routine and Organization

People with ADHD often struggle with time management, organization, and completing tasks. Establishing routines and organization strategies can help alleviate these challenges.

Consider using tools such as a planner or digital apps to stay organized and keep track of your to-dos, deadlines, and appointments. Structure your environment to minimize distractions–organize your workspace, and keep noise to a minimum if that helps. Also, break down larger tasks into smaller, manageable chunks to prevent overwhelm.

10.6. Foster Positive Relationships

Positive and understanding relationships can be a powerful antidote to the stressors life presents. A supportive social network can provide emotional support, practical assistance, and positive affirmation which can help manage ADHD symptoms.

Consider joining ADHD support groups, either in person or online. The camaraderie of individuals with similar experiences can be immensely comforting and encouraging. Alternatively, turn to trusted family members or friends and let them know what kind of support you need.

10.7. Cultivate a Positive Self-Approach

Remember, ADHD is a part of you, but it does not define you. Developing a positive self-identity is crucial for your mental well-being.

It's okay to have bad days. Don't beat yourself up. Instead, practice self-compassion. Recognize your strengths and accomplishments, no matter how small they may seem. Seek professional help if you struggle with feelings of guilt, depression, or low self-esteem.

10.8. Engage in Enjoyable Activities

Finding activities you enjoy can serve as an outlet for stress and also improve your mood. Music, art, sports, gardening–find what resonates with you and engage in it regularly.

In closing, remember this–your journey with ADHD is unique. What works for one person may not work for you. Explore different strategies. Experiment, experience, and embrace the journey towards nourishing your resilience and overall well-being.

Chapter 11. Support and Resources: Where to Seek Help

Navigating the world with ADHD can be challenging, and the journey feels less intimidating when you are not alone. The strength of community support, professional guidance, and various resources at your disposal can be invaluable.

11.1. Understanding the Professional Landscape

Before we understand where to seek help, it is crucial to acknowledge the diverse group of professionals available for assistance.

1. **Psychiatrists** specialize in mental health, including substance use disorders. They can diagnose ADHD with precision, prescribe medications, and offer psychotherapy.

2. **Psychologists** are professionals specializing in diagnosing and treating diseases of the brain, emotional disturbance, and behavior problems.

3. **Mental Health Counselors** are trained to diagnose and provide individual and group counseling.

4. **Social Workers** can offer case management and hospital discharge planning, as well as work as an advocate for patients and their family.

5. **Family Therapists** review familial patterns of behavior as they influence the individual living with ADHD.

6. **Registered Dietitians** can advise on a proper diet that can

improve brain health.

11.2. Seeking Professional Help

Starting therapy can be an empowering decision, but the task of finding the most suitable therapist can be overwhelming. Here are a few steps to streamline the process:

1. Determine what kind of professional help you need.

2. Consult your insurance provider about mental health services coverage.

3. Seek out recommendations from your doctor, friends, or trustworthy online resources.

4. Spend some time researching potential therapists, their experience, qualifications, and approaches to understand who could be a good fit.

5. Schedule meetings with potential therapists to assess if the comfort level and promise of efficacy exist.

11.3. ADHD Support Groups

Joining a support group can have a transformative impact on individuals with ADHD and their caregivers. They can serve as a solace, reassurance, and offer experiential advice and strategies which a professional might not provide. Online platforms like ADDA (ADHD Adults), CHADD (Children and Adults with ADHD), and ADHD Foundation provide resources and aid in finding local support groups.

11.4. Schools and Educators

Teachers play fundamental roles in facilitating the academic success of children with ADHD. Educational strategies, accommodations via an Individualized Education Program (IEP) or a Section 504 plan, can allay many challenges linked with ADHD. Reach out to school representatives and special education coordinators to understand how best to navigate the academic path with ADHD.

11.5. Online Resources

The Internet is a treasure trove of resources that cover almost every ADHD-related subject under the sun. A few notable resources include:

1. ADDitude : A prominent magazine and online resource that offers expert advice, helpful tips, the latest news, and inspiring stories about ADHD.

2. The ADHD Handbook : A comprehensive online manual offering information about diagnosis and treatment options, aimed at parents, educators, and health care providers.

3. Understood : An online platform dedicated to offering support to families of children struggling with learning and attention issues. It provides expert advice, personalized resources, and access to a supportive online community.

11.6. Books and Other Publications

Many books can offer both general knowledge about ADHD and unique lived experiences. A few recommended readings include:

1. **Driven to Distraction** by Edward M. Hallowell and John J. Ratey, groundbreaking and comprehensive look at ADHD.

2. **Smart but Scattered** by Peg Dawson and Richard Guare, focuses on improving executive skills.

3. **Taking Charge of ADHD** by Russell A. Barkley, offers science-based guidance for parents.

11.7. Navigating Medications and Other Treatments

Understanding ADHD medications and their side effects involves communicating effectively with healthcare providers. Try keeping track of symptoms, any side effects, and the impact on general well-being during medication trials. There are also various non-pharmacologic treatments available such as cognitive-behavioral therapy, ADHD coaching, neurofeedback, which can be explored as per individual suitability.

11.8. Advocacy and Legal Assistance

Know your rights or the rights of your child. Several legislations protect individuals with ADHD, both in the workplace and educational institutions. Organizations like CHADD and ADHD Foundation also provide resources pertinent to legalities related to ADHD.

In conclusion, the landscape for ADHD support and resources is extensive and varied, catering to different needs and preferences. Navigating this landscape might seem daunting initially, but remember, reaching out for help is itself a major step forward on your well-being journey.